# How Henny Hatched Her Eggs

By Melissa Kolb

For my own babies who inspire me everyday:
Quinton, Lacey, & Natalie

Miss. Henny stood and waited.

In fact, she waited all day long.

She looked them over, up and down.

It appeared that nothing was wrong.

She brought them mouthfuls of tasty worms,

some sweet leaves,
and water to drink.

She did everything a good mother would do,

At least everything **she** could think.

Miss. Lucy had six chicks.

Miss. Sally had nine.

Miss. Fanny had eleven,

And this was her first time.

The chicks in nests around her,
Quickly numbered over a ton.

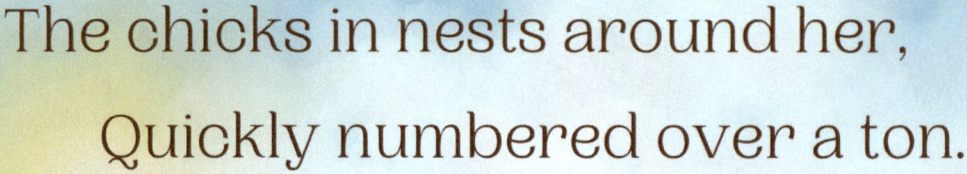

The other hens had so many,
But Miss. Henny still had none.

Her mama tried to tell her.

She hated to see her daughter struggle.

There was such a simple answer there,
But Henny had too many thoughts to juggle.

Exhausted from her unending confusion,
                Her trouble and her toil,

"What else can I do?" She wondered.

"I can't leave them in the sun, **they'll spoil.**"

Thirty-six unhatched eggs.

No movements. No sounds.

"Maybe they need some fertilizer?"

""Perhaps to be rolled around?"

She tried everything at least twice.
Could this be a dud batch?

It was time for professional advice.

"Mama, why won't my little chicks hatch?"

Her mama's words were direct and gentle.

She was never one to condemn.

Criticizing would not be helpful. She simply asked,

The END

## About the Author /Illustrator:

Hello! I'm Melissa and this is the real Henny. At the time of this publication, we have 31 chickens on our small hobby farm. The most we've had at one time was 50! With that many chickens running around, I've learned quite a bit about them over the years. For one, they aren't the smartest animals in the world, but that's what makes them really fun to watch. They sometimes act pretty silly.

Did you know that when a hen lays her eggs, she'll cluck really loudly for a couple of minutes afterwards? It's almost as if she's celebrating...... or maybe she's bragging to the other hens. I mean come on, she hasn't even hatched the baby chicks yet and she wants a round of applause!? That gave me the idea for this book.

Henny was too proud to ask for advice when she couldn't figure out how to hatch her eggs. She ended up wasting a lot of time and looked quite silly in the process. If you have any pets, maybe you could write your own story about them and the silly things they do. I hope I get to read it someday.

Copyright © 2023 Homespun Stories Press, Melissa Kolb
Homespun Stories Press - Maryville, TN 37803

All rights reserved. No part of this book may be reproduced or used in any manner without the prior written permission of the copyright owner, except for the use of brief quotations in a book review.
To request permissions, contact the publisher at homespunstoriespress@gmail.com

Publisher's Cataloging-in-Publication data

Names: Kolb, Melissa, author.
Title: How Henny Hatched Her Eggs / written and illustrated by Melissa Kolb.
Description: Maryville, TN: Homespun Stories Press, 2023. | First Edition: November 2023

Summary: Henny is a determined chicken with dreams of motherhood. She can't wait to hatch a batch of her own chicks, but she isn't sure what they need to succeed and tries various comical attempts.

Identifiers: LCCN: 2023920761
ISBN: 978-1-962512-04-6 (hardcover) | 978-1-962512-03-9 (paperback) | 978-1-962512-05-3 (ebook)

Subjects: LCSH Chickens--Juvenile fiction. | Farm animals--Juvenile fiction. | BISAC JUVENILE FICTION / Animals / Farm Animals | JUVENILE FICTION / Animals / Birds | JUVENILE FICTION / Readers / Beginner
Classification: LCC PZ7.1 .K65 Ho 2023 | DDC [E]--dc23

Visit us at: HomespunStoriesPress.com

Made in the USA
Las Vegas, NV
04 December 2023